AF605420

ARCTIC OCEAN
SEVERNAYA ZEMLYA
FRANZ JOSEF
NEW SIBERIAN ISLANDS
Wrangel Island
FINLAND
RUSSIA
ESTONIA
LATVIA
LITHUANIA
BELARUS
UKRAINE
MOLDOVA
ROMANIA
BULGARIA
GEORGIA
KAZAKHSTAN
MONGOLIA
UZBEKISTAN
KRYGYSTAN
TAJIKISTAN
TURKMENISTAN
ARMENIA
AZERBAIJAN
GREECE
TURKEY
CYPRUS
SYRIA
IRAQ
IRAN
AFGHANISTAN
PAKISTAN
JORDAN
KUWAIT
EGYPT
SAUDI ARABIA
QATAR
UNITED ARAB EMIRATES
OMAN
YEMEN
ERITREA
SUDAN
DJIBOUTI
ETHIOPIA
SOMALIA
KENYA
UGANDA
DEM. REP OF THE CONGO
RWANDA
BURUNDI
TANZANIA
MALAWI
ZAMBIA
MOZAMBIQUE
ZIMBABWE
BOTSWANA
SOUTH AFRICA
LESOTHO
SWAZILAND
MADAGASCAR
COMOROS
SEYCHELLES
MAURITIUS
REUNION
MALDIVES
SRI LANKA
INDIA
NEPAL
BANGLADESH
CHINA
NORTH KOREA
SOUTH KOREA
JAPAN
MYANMAR (BURMA)
LAOS
THAILAND
CAMBODIA
VIETNAM
PHILIPPINES
ADAMAN ISLANDS (INDIA)
NICOBAR ISLANDS (INDIA)
MALAYSIA
BRUNEI
INDONESIA
PAPUA NEW GUINEA
GUAM
FEDERATED STATES OF MICRONESIA
MARSHALL ISLANDS
KIRIBATI
SOLOMON ISLANDS
TUVALU
SAMOA
VANUATU
FIJI
TONGA
NEW CALEDONIA (FRANCE)
NORTH PACIFIC OCEAN
INDIAN OCEAN
AUSTRALIA
NEW ZEALAND
PRINCE EDWARD ISLANDS
ILES CROZET (FRANCE)
KERGUELEN ISLAND (FRANCE)

GLOBETROTTERS
CANADA
Jane Hinchey
REDBACK
publishing

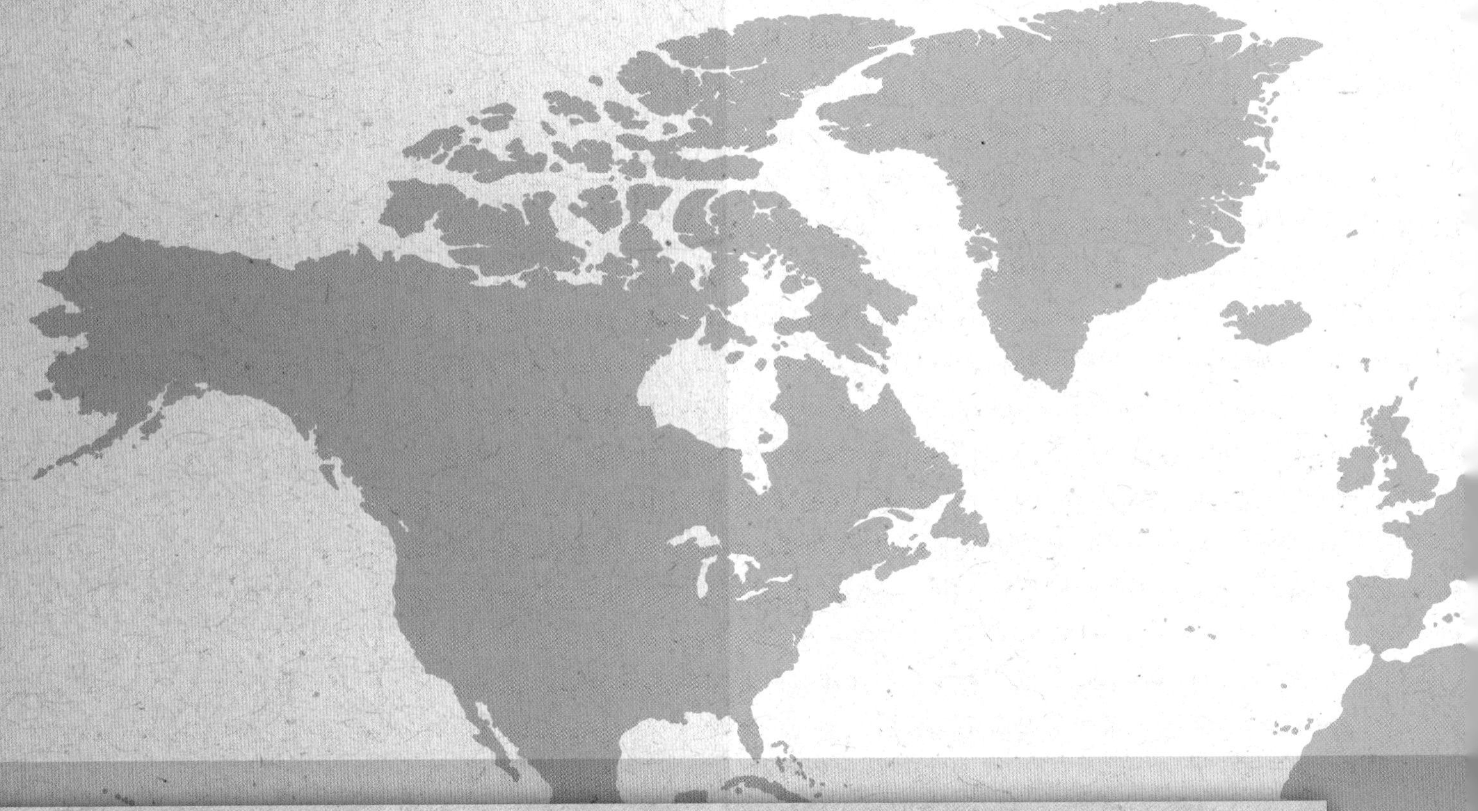

First Published 2022 by
Redback Publishing
PO Box 357 Frenchs Forest NSW 2086
Australia

www.redbackpublishing.com
orders@redbackpublishing.com

ISBN 978-1-922322-42-5

Author: Jane Hinchey
Editor: Marlene Vaughan
Design: Redback Publishing

Original illustrations © Redback Publishing 2022
Originated by Redback Publishing

Printed and bound in Malaysia

Acknowledgements
Abbreviations: l—left, r—right, b—bottom, t—top, c—centre, m—middle
We would like to thank the following for permission to reproduce photographs: (Images © shutterstock) p9br by Shaun Jeffers/Shutterstock, p11bl by Gregory Johnston/Shutterstock, p12tl Ansgar Walk via Wikipedia, p13t Frank E. Kleinschmidt via Wikipedia, p15 Raph_PH via Wikipedia, p16bl Timkal via Wikipedia, p18tl Jeff Whyte/Shutterstock, p18br Ric Jacyno/Shutterstock, p18bl vladdon/Shutterstock, p19tr Vincent JIANG/Shutterstock, p20tl Denis Pepin/Shutterstock, p20bl Mike Broglio/Shutterstock, p21tl Iurii Osadchi/Shutterstock, p21bl Scott Prokop/Shutterstock, p24 Lou Stejskal/Shutterstock, p24bl Featureflash Photo Agency/Shutterstock, p24br Christian Bertrand/Shutterstock, p25tr Featureflash Photo Agency/Shutterstock, p25br Tom Rose/Shutterstock, p26bl By i viewfinder/Shutterstock.

Every effort has been made to contact copyright holders of any material reproduced in this book. Any omissions will be rectified in subsequent printings if notice is given to the publisher.

A catalogue record for this book is available from the National Library of Australia

CONTENTS

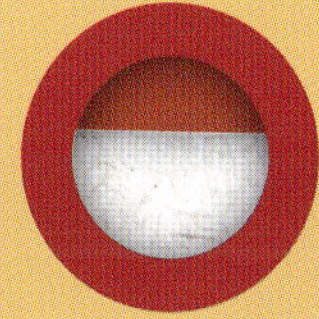

MAP OF CANADA

Find Them on a Map!

Canada has 13 provinces and territories. They are:

- Alberta
- British Columbia
- Manitoba
- New Brunswick
- Newfoundland and Labrador
- Northwest Territories
- Nova Scotia
- Nunavut
- Ontario
- Prince Edward Island
- Quebec
- Saskatchewan
- Yukon

SNAPSHOT

COUNTRY	Canada
CAPITAL	Ottawa
OFFICIAL LANGUAGES	English and French
AREA	9,984,670 square kilometres
POPULATION	38,060,280 (2021)
OFFICIAL RELIGION	None
CURRENCY	Canadian dollar

Canada

Yukon

Northwest Territories

British Columbia

Alberta

Saskatchewan

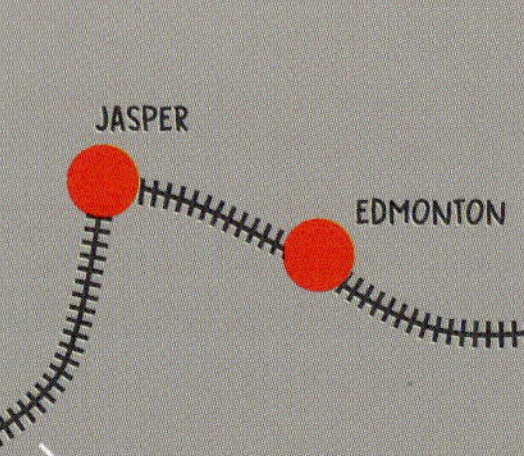

JASPER

EDMONTON

SASKATOON

KAMLOOPS

VANCOUVER

UNITED STATES OF AMERICA

Did You Know?

Canada is home to one of the world's greatest train journeys. You can travel from coast to coast on the Canada Rail, all the way from Vancouver to Toronto. The Canadian takes four days and four nights to cross 4,466 kilometres, travelling through some of the most beautiful scenery in the world.

Aurora Borealis
YELLOWKNIFE NATIONAL PARK

Fairmont Le Chateau Frontenac
OLD QUEBEC CITY

DENMARK
CONDUCTOR
Nunavut
Manitoba
Ontario
Quebec
Newfoundland and Labrador
Prince Edward Island
New Brunswick
Nova Scotia
WINNIPEG
TORONTO

WELCOME TO CANADA

The region has been inhabited for tens of thousands of years and Canada is a politically stable country, with a rich and vibrant cultural life and high standard of living.

Canada is the second-largest country in the world. It is located in North America, above the United States of America. Despite its size, it is one of the most sparsely populated countries. Apart from its land border shared with the USA, it is surrounded by water, with the Atlantic Ocean in the east, the Pacific Ocean in the west and the Arctic Ocean in the North. It is a geographically diverse country, with stunning mountain ranges, rolling plains and valleys, pristine lakes, and the longest coastline in the world. Forests cover approximately half of the country's total area.

Montreal - the largest city in Canada's Quebec province

Did You Know?

The Canada-US border is 8,891 kilometres long, making it the longest international border in the world.

PEOPLE

Canada is a multicultural country, with a population of around 31 million people. Canada's First Nations people lived there long before it was settled by the French and British. More recently, immigrants from all over Europe, Asia, and South America have arrived in Canada, adding to its diversity.

Did You Know?

The Vikings were the first Europeans to visit North America, making it as far as Nova Scotia and Newfoundland on Canada's eastern seaboard. Evidence suggests that the Vikings left North America approximately 1,000 years ago when the climate became too cold to sustain cattle farming. Many scientists believe this mini-Ice Age drove the Vikings to seek settlement in warmer lands.

L'Anse aux Meadows is the first and only known site established by Vikings in North America

IN A NUTSHELL

Natural Resources

Canada's natural resources include wood, petroleum, coal, iron ore, potash, nickel, copper, zinc and lead.

Tugboat pushing boom of freshly cut logs to the mill for processing

Agriculture

Canada produces crops such as grain, wheat, barley, oats, rye, corn (maize), potatoes, white beans and mixed grains as well as livestock, dairy and poultry, fish and horticulture.

Main Industries

Canada's most important industry is real estate. Other important industries include energy, mining, technology, manufacturing and agriculture.

GOVERNMENT

Canada is a democratic country and Members of Parliament are elected by the people of Canada.

There are three levels of government:

- Federal
- Provincial
- Municipal

Why Does Canada Have a Queen?

Canada's government is a constitutional monarchy, based on the British Westminster system. The British Monarch is Head of State and represented in Canada by the Governor General.

FIRST NATIONS

Indigenous Squamish woman

Canada's First Nations people have lived in the region for more than 30,000 years. Today, there are over 1.67 million people who identify as Aboriginal or Indigenous Canadians. First Nations peoples, Métis and Inuit peoples make up over 630 communities that represent over 50 nations and speak in over 50 languages.

Fast Fact

Just under six per cent of Canadians have Aboriginal ancestry. About half of all First Nations people live on reserves all across Canada. These reserves can be very different geographical areas and this creates vast differences in the daily lives of Canadian First Nations peoples.

Native North Americans built teepee tents with an open top to draw the fire smoke out

Kwakwaka'wakw

The Kwakwaka'wakw people live in the Pacific Northwest. Today there are over 5,500 Kwakwaka'wakw, across 17 tribes. The preservation of the Kwakwaka'wakw's cultural and spiritual practice is very important, with language, song and story telling and dance playing an essential modern role. The Kwakwaka'wakw are fishermen and hunters and highly skilled wood carvers. Totem poles are especially significant and usually carved from the tall trunks of Western Redcedar trees.

Kwakiutl men in ceremonial coats

First Nations communities hold powwows to celebrate and showcase Indigenous dance, music, food, arts and crafts.

Cree

The largest First Nations population is the Cree. The Cree people are nomadic, moving across large areas with the seasons. Today, about 120,000 Cree can be found throughout Canada.

INUIT PEOPLE

Inuit people wearing traditional seal fur clothing in the freezing climate

The Inuit people make up less than 10 per cent of the Indigenous population. They arrived in North America about 4,000 years ago, settling in the region's Arctic area. In 1999, the territory of Nunavut was created as part of a treaty settlement with the Canadian government, making it the largest and northernmost territory.

Ulukhaktok, an Inuit settlement in Canada

The Inuit adapted to the harsh landscape, hunting fish, seals, caribou (reindeer) and birds for food. In the past, Inuit people sometimes lived in igloos, called iglu, but they now live in houses.

The Igloo

Igloo walls are made from blocks of ice that protect from the extreme temperatures

Community of igloos in an Inuit village

Animal skins keep the inhabitants warm

Traditionally, in winter Inuit people lived in snow packed huts. In some regions these were dome shaped and large enough to house up to twenty people. Often, multiple huts were joined so communities could connect. There were even spaces for their dogs. People kept warm inside using animal skins and furs. These igloos remain culturally important to the Inuit people, with young people even learning how to build igloos at school.

LANGUAGE

Canada has two distinct regions – French Canada and English Canada. There are 10 million French speakers in Canada, but most of them live in Quebec, the largest of the ten provinces. For the Québécois, French is their first language. The rest of Canada speaks English as their official language, although many English-speaking Canadians also study French.

Petit Champlain Street in the French Canada region in Quebec

Nearly five million Canadians speak a language other than French or English. Many of these people are immigrants from elsewhere in the world, who continue speaking their own mother tongue.

Other languages spoken in Canada include:

Indigenous Languages

In Canada, there are twelve Indigenous language families made up of 70 different languages. Many of these languages are at risk, with only 15 per cent of First Nations people speaking their heritage language. The UNESCO Atlas of the World's Languages in Danger project reports that only the most widely spoken Indigenous languages, Cree, Inuktitut and Ojibwa have enough speakers to sustain them.

Language is an important part of cultural identity and there are many programs now teaching Indigenous languages to young people.

Fast Fact

Cree is spoken by approximately 120,000 individuals, making it the most common indigenous language in Canada.

Paul McCartney from the 'Beatles'

Did You Know?

In 2019, students at Allison Bernard Memorial High School in Eskasoni First Nation, Cape Breton translated the Beatles' song *Blackbird* into Mi'kmaq, and recorded it with Emma Stevens singing. The purpose was to draw attention to the danger of Indigenous languages dying out. It went viral, receiving high praise from many public figures, including the songwriter Sir Paul McCartney.

LIVING IN CANADA

Richmond Hill in Ontario, Canada

Canada is a huge country, but over 90 per cent of the population lives in towns and cities in the south, close to the border with the United States. Over half of the population lives in the provinces of Ontario and Quebec.

Sachs Harbour

Rural Areas

Canada's vast wilderness areas make up 60 per cent of the country, with sparsely populated areas. Small populations of Canadians live in the Northwest Territories, where extreme weather conditions have made settlement more difficult.

Sachs Harbour is the northernmost community in the Northwest Territories. It has a population of about 100 people and is over 500 kilometres from Inuvik, where most of its supplies must come from.

Did You Know?

Canada is so large that it spans across six time zones.

Towns and Cities

The most densely populated areas are Vancouver, Calgary, Edmonton, the Great Toronto area, Ottawa and Montreal. Canadian people who live in cities or urban areas enjoy a high quality of life. Residents have access to excellent infrastructure, shopping, markets and restaurants. People play sports, visit galleries and museums and attend events. Families can choose from good schools and medical facilities, and children have quite a lot of freedom and independence from a young age.

Aerial view of Montreal showing the Biosphere Environment Museum and Saint Lawrence River

Fun Fact

The city of Old Québec is a UNESCO World Heritage treasure.

Frontenac Castle Opened in 1893 in Old Quebec City

DAILY LIFE

Canada is one of the wealthiest countries in the world and the standard of living is generally very high. Canadians have access to excellent healthcare, education and infrastructure.

Being a large country, there is much to do and experience. Canadians are well-known for their love of outdoor pursuits and sport. They savour their leisure time and cultural pursuits. All over the country, people belong to cultural and sports clubs.

Transport

Canada has safe and efficient transport systems. Public transport is excellent in all major cities and urban areas. Train and bus networks spread right across the country for long distance travel, although because of the vast distances, many people choose to fly.

Train travelling through the Rocky Mountains

In Canada, family is very important. Most households consist of a nuclear family, but it is common for extended families to come together to share special occasions.

Religion

When the French and British colonised Canada, they brought their religions with them. The French were Catholic while the British were primarily Protestants. Today almost 70 per cent of Canadians identify as Catholic or Protestant.

There are smaller communities of Muslims, Sikhs, Hindus, and Buddhists. Canada has the fourth largest Jewish community in the world.

Annual Leave

In Canada, each state or province sets the amount of leave workers are entitled to. Some provinces allow workers to take two weeks paid vacation, but most grant three to four weeks.

Banff National Park is great for a getaway

A LOVE OF SPORTS

Canadians love sport. Due to the alpine terrain, snow sports are extremely popular. Skiing, snowboarding and other winter sports are not only popular with locals, but account for a major share of tourism. Visitors come from all over the world to experience Canada's famous ski-resorts. The Whistler National Park attracts people all year round, with mountain biking and hiking being very popular in the summer months.

Other popular sports include basketball, soccer, baseball, curling, tennis and football. Canada has two national sports: **ice hockey and lacrosse**.

Lacrosse - also called the fastest game on two feet

Canada's Summer Sports

Canada's First Nations people have been playing the sport now known as lacrosse for over 500 years. Today, it remains an important cultural activity for the country's First Nations people and is also played by tens of thousands of other Canadians. In 1994, it was officially designated Canada's national summer sport.

Canada won gold at the 2014 Olympic Games

Ice Hockey

(just called 'hockey' in Canada)

Canada's most popular sport is hockey. Over 600,000 Canadians are registered to play hockey, while many more unregistered players take part in the sport. Those who don't play, still follow the National Hockey League (NHL), a professional hockey league that includes teams from both Canada and the United States.

There are seven NHL teams in Canada: :

- Calgary Flames
- Edmonton Oilers
- Montreal Canadiens
- Ottawa Senators
- Toronto Maple Leafs
- Vancouver Canucks
- Winnipeg Jets

Huge stadium where hundreds of people come to watch

EDUCATION

Canada's education system is well funded and is one of the best in the world, with over 90 per cent of Canadians finishing high school. Provincial and territorial governments are responsible for their own school systems, so there are some differences across different states, but the standard is high right across the country.

Simon Fraser University from above

A new Canadian elementary school

Fast Fact

There are 4.92 million primary school children in Canada and 2.15 million students at universities and colleges.

There are four stages of schooling in Canada: pre-primary education, primary education, secondary education and post-secondary or tertiary education. School attendance is mandatory until the age of 16 in all provinces except for Manitoba, Ontario, and New Brunswick where the required age is 18.

In primary school, students have one teacher for the whole year. Subjects include mathematics, reading, science, geography, music, physical education, and the arts. Language arts are taught in French in Quebec and in English everywhere else.

Inside an art classroom in Toronto

The school year starts in August and ends in June. Students who attend public schools don't wear school uniforms.

FAMOUS CANADIANS

Canada has a thriving arts scene, which has produced many famous faces in the film, television, and music industries.

Justin Bieber

Born in Ontario, Bieber released his first album at the age of 15 and went on to world superstardom.

Ryan Reynolds

Born in Vancouver, Reynolds has starred in many box office hits including the Deadpool series.

Drake

Grammy award winning rapper Drake is from Toronto.

James Cameron

This proud Canadian has directed some of the most successful films in history, including Titanic and Avatar.

Joni Mitchell

Joni Mitchell was a poet who taught herself guitar and went on to become one of the most successful musicians of the 1960s and 1970s and an icon in the years since.

Shawn Mendes

Shawn Mendes was born in Toronto. He rose to fame with his first single, *Life of the Party*, and he now has many fans all around the world.

FOOD

Canadian food varies from region to region, but meat, poultry, fish and vegetables are widely enjoyed by all. Rich soil provides abundant grains, fruits, and vegetables. Mealtimes are important and seen as a time to relax, savour food and enjoy the company of others.

Canadian cuisine is influenced by its multicultural communities and restaurants serve fare from all over the world. At the heart of much of its cuisine is the country's Anglo-Gallic influences.

An abundance of fresh food is available at the markets in Vancouver

Two Favourite Foods!

A bowl of poutine in a French Canadian bistro

Potatoes

The dish called Poutine originated in Quebec and consists of French fries and cheese curd covered in gravy. It's now popular all around the country. Another potato comfort food is Scalloped Potatoes, where thinly sliced potatoes are baked in a creamy mixture of butter, milk, and flour. Delicious!

Maple

It's the national tree and the symbol is on the national flag. It's official, Canadians love their maple ... including maple syrup. There's nothing more Canadian than pancakes topped with maple syrup.

GEOGRAPHY & WILDLIFE

Canada is a geographically diverse country, with stunning mountain ranges, rolling plains and valleys, more than two million lakes and the longest coastline in the world.

The country spans a massive 5,500 kilometres from east to west, and 4,600 kilometres from north to south. In the south, it shares an 8,892-kilometre-long border with the United States. Apart from its shared land border in the south, it is surrounded by water. The Atlantic Ocean meets the east coast, the Pacific Ocean meets the west and the Arctic Ocean meets the northern edge of the country.

Climate

The Canadian climate varies depending on the region, but is generally temperate. In the southern regions, the warmest temperatures are during July and August, and winters can be very cold. In the northern part of the country, temperatures only rise above freezing during summer.

Majestic Mountains

Dramatic and beautiful, Canada has 21,324 recognised mountains. The tallest is Mount Logan at 5,959 metres high.

Forests cover approximately half of the country's total area and are home to a diverse range of animals. Canada has icy arctic environments, vast grasslands and marine and freshwater regions. There are many rich and varied habitats where species of moose, buffalo, wild horses, wolf, cougar, coyote, deer, birds and fish can thrive. However, since 1970, 59 per cent of species have seen a decline in numbers and many are now on the country's endangered animal list. There are many programs protecting Canada's natural environments and its wildlife.

The pileated woodpecker lives in the boreal forests of Canada

Canada is home to three bear species:

- The polar bear
- The black bear
- The grizzly bear

AMAZING PLACES

Lake Louise

Lake Louise is a hamlet in Banff National Park in the Canadian Rockies. It's known for its turquoise, glacier-fed lake, ringed by high peaks and overlooked by a stately chateau.

Aurora Borealis

Yellowknife is the best place in the world to view the Aurora Borealis, also known as the Northern Lights. The phenomenon is caused by the aurora belt, an electromagnetic field floating like a halo over the Earth, hundreds of kilometres above the North Pole.

Niagara Falls

The amazing Niagara Falls is renowned for its beauty and is the collective name for three waterfalls that straddle the international border between Canada and the US.

FLAG AND SYMBOLS

National Anthem

The national anthem of Canada is named *O Canada* by Calixa Lavallée.

Flag

The National Flag of Canada has three vertical panels; the two smaller side panels are red and the centre panel is white with a red maple leaf. It has served as a Canadian symbol since the 18th century.

National Tree

Canada's national tree is the maple.

National Pattern

The Maple Leaf Tartan is Canada's national pattern.

Did You Know?

There is no national flower of Canada but each of the provinces and territories has an official floral emblem.

National Animal

Canada's national animal is the beaver. It is also the national symbol.

GLOSSARY

culture practices, beliefs and customs of a society or people

dialect variation of a language unique to a region

endangered when a species is at risk

First Nations group of Indigenous people of the same language and cultural beliefs.

igloo culturally important, snow packed huts that the Inuit people lived in

immigrant person who settles in another country

poutine dish that originated in Quebec and consists of French fries and cheese curd covered in gravy

Vikings Norse people who voyaged around Europe and North America from the 8th to the late 11th centuries

INDEX

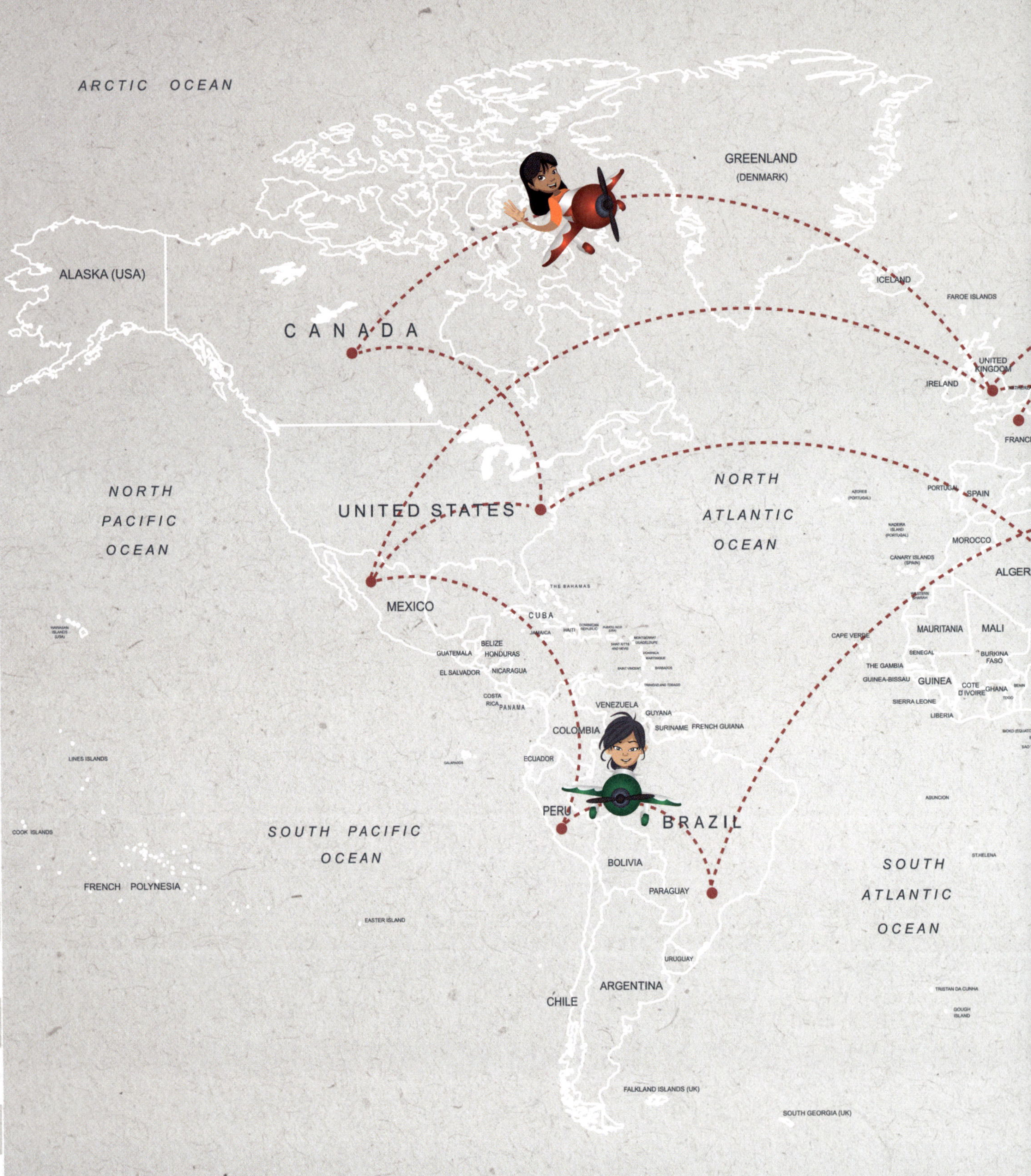
ARCTIC OCEAN
GREENLAND
(DENMARK)
ALASKA (USA)
CANADA
ICELAND
FAROE ISLANDS
UNITED KINGDOM
IRELAND
FRANCE
NORTH PACIFIC OCEAN
UNITED STATES
NORTH ATLANTIC OCEAN
PORTUGAL
SPAIN
MOROCCO
ALGERI
MEXICO
CUBA
MAURITANIA
MALI
CAPE VERDE
BELIZE
GUATEMALA
HONDURAS
EL SALVADOR
NICARAGUA
COSTA RICA
PANAMA
SENEGAL
THE GAMBIA
BURKINA FASO
GUINEA-BISSAU
GUINEA
COTE D'IVOIRE
GHANA
SIERRA LEONE
LIBERIA
VENEZUELA
GUYANA
SURINAME
FRENCH GUIANA
COLOMBIA
ECUADOR
LINES ISLANDS
PERU
BRAZIL
SOUTH PACIFIC OCEAN
COOK ISLANDS
BOLIVIA
FRENCH POLYNESIA
PARAGUAY
SOUTH ATLANTIC OCEAN
EASTER ISLAND
URUGUAY
ARGENTINA
CHILE
FALKLAND ISLANDS (UK)
SOUTH GEORGIA (UK)